976.2
FOR

Foran, Jill
Nebraska

34880000823380

NEBRASKA

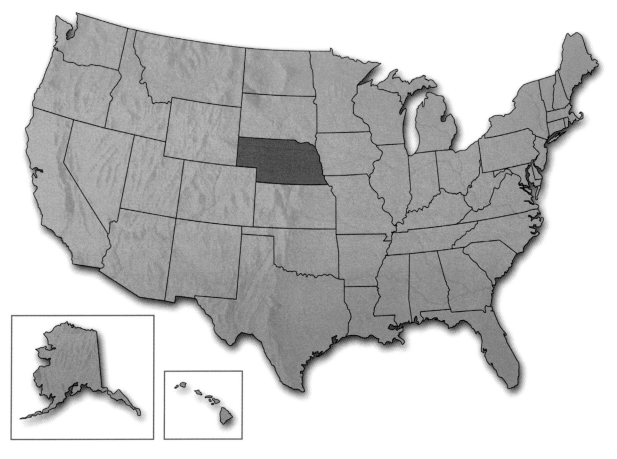

Jill Foran

Published by Weigl Publishers Inc.
123 South Broad Street, Box 227
Mankato, MN   56002
USA
Web site: http://www.weigl.com

Library of Congress Cataloging-in-Publication Data

Foran, Jill
   Nebraska / Jill Foran.
      p. cm. -- (A kid's guide to American states)
   Includes index.
   ISBN 1-930954-97-2 (lib. bdg.)
    1. Nebraska--Juvenile literature. [1. Nebraska.] I. Title. II. Series.

F666.3 .F67 2001

                                             2001026001

ISBN 1-930954-88-3 (pbk.)

Printed in the United States of America
1 2 3 4 5 6 7 8 9 10   05 04 03 02 01

Project Coordinator
Jennifer Nault
Substantive Editor
Rennay Craats
Copy Editor
Heather Kissock
Designers
Warren Clark
Terry Paulhus
Photo Researcher
Angela Lowen

Photograph Credits

Every reasonable effort has been made to trace ownership and to obtain
permission to reprint copyright material. The publishers would be
pleased to have any errors or omissions brought to their attention so
that they may be corrected in subsequent printings.

Cover: Native American Dancer (Marilyn "Angel" Wynn), Corn with Husk (Corel Corporation),
Ak-Sar-Ben Rodeo: page 28R; **Archive Photos:** page 22MR; **Kent C. Behrens:** page 23B;
Burwell Area Convention and Visitor's Bureau: page 26BR; **Terry L. Cartwright:** page 15MR;
Corbis Corporation: pages 5T, 8T, 8BR; **Corel Corporation:** pages 3T, 4BL, 11MR, 16BL;
Defense Visual Information Center: page 15MR; **Michael Forsberg:** page 4T; **Mark E.
Gibson/The Image Finders:** page 15ML; **Greater Omaha Convention and Visitor's Bureau:**
page 25B; **Lincoln/Lancaster County Convention and Visitor's Bureau:** page 20T; **Steve
Mulligan Photography:** pages 5BR, 6BR, 9T, 10T, 11ML, 12BR, 19B; **National Museum of
Roller Skating:** page 26BL; **Nebraska Department of Economic Development, Division of
Travel and Tourism:** pages 4BR, 6T, 6BL, 7T, 7B, 8BR, 9M, 9B, 10B, 11B, 12BL, 13T, 15B, 17B,
18T, 18B, 20B, 21BR, 28L, 29R; **Nebraska State Historical Society:** pages 16T, 16BR, 17T, 19T;
Omaha Lancers Hockey Team: page 27BL; **Omaha Symphony:** page 24T; **Omaha Theater
Company for Young People:** page 24BR; **PhotoDisc:** pages 13B, 14B; **Photofest:** pages 21BL,
24BL, 26T; **Stuhr Museum of the Prairie Pioneer:** page 12T; **Union Pacific Historical
Collection:** pages 3M, 14T; **University of Nebraska, Lied Center for Performing Arts:** pages 3B,
25T; **University of Nebraska Lincoln Photo Services:** pages 27T, 27BR; **Wausa Community
Swedish Smorgasbord/Sandra Lang:** page 22T; **P. Michael Whyte:** page 21T; **Wilbur Czech
Museum:** pages 22T, 22B, **Marilyn "Angel" Wynn:** page 23T.

CONTENTS

INTRODUCTION

Farmers depend on Nebraska's Platte River for irrigation water.

Nebraska is a state in the Midwest. It lies halfway between the Atlantic and Pacific Oceans. The Platte River flows across the state, offering its waters for **irrigation**, recreation, and the production of **hydroelectric** power. The Platte's broad valley is an important transportation **corridor**, linking eastern and western Nebraska. It has provided a path for thousands of travelers throughout history. The river is also responsible for the state's name. The Oto, who were among the first Native Peoples to live in the area, named the Platte River *Nebrathka*, which means "flat water."

Nebraska is nicknamed "The Cornhusker State," after its main agricultural crop. Corn grows in many parts of the state. Large wheat fields, cornfields, and vast grazing lands have earned Nebraska the reputation as one of the world's best farming regions.

QUICK FACTS

The state capital of Nebraska is Lincoln.

Nebraska covers an area of about 77,358 square miles.

Nebraska became the thirty-seventh state in the Union on March 1, 1867.

Corn grows on 8.3 million acres of land in Nebraska.

More than 1 million passengers use the Omaha Airport every year.

With about 1.7 million people, Nebraska ranks as the thirty-eighth state in population.

The state song is "Beautiful Nebraska."

Every stream and river in Nebraska eventually drains into the Missouri River.

Getting There

Nebraska is bordered by six other states. South Dakota is to the north of Nebraska, while Iowa and Missouri are to the east. Kansas lies to the south, and Colorado and Wyoming are to the west. The Missouri River forms Nebraska's entire eastern border and part of its northern border.

Nebraska's central location makes it easy to reach. It is within a one-day drive of many major cities, including Chicago, St. Louis, Kansas City, Minneapolis, Denver, and Salt Lake City. Many interstate highways run through the state. Interstate 80, an east-west route running across Nebraska, is one of the state's busiest highways. Several rail lines cross the state, and passenger trains serve the larger cities. Nebraska also has more than two hundred airports for those who prefer air travel. The busiest airport in the state is in Omaha.

Nebraska Location Map

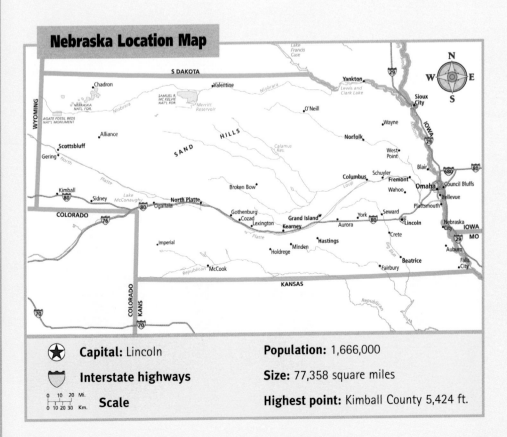

⭐ **Capital:** Lincoln

🛡 **Interstate highways**

Scale 0 10 20 Mi. / 0 10 20 30 Km.

Population: 1,666,000

Size: 77,358 square miles

Highest point: Kimball County 5,424 ft.

Today, people can take a covered wagon tour of the Oregon Trail, and retrace the route of the early settlers.

QUICK FACTS

The goldenrod is the state flower.

The cottonwood is Nebraska's state tree. It was chosen over Nebraska's elm trees because many of the state's elms had been killed by Dutch elm disease.

The state insect of Nebraska is the honeybee.

The western meadowlark is Nebraska's state bird.

In the early nineteenth century, several thousand travelers trekked through Nebraska. The Platte River Valley became a westward route as countless pioneers from the east headed for the rich farmland of Oregon and the gold mines of California. The Oregon, California, and Mormon trails were all very important routes that followed the Platte River.

At this time, Nebraska was regarded as little more than an access route to the west. Pioneers traveled through the region, mistakenly assuming that the dry land would be difficult to farm. The region was flat, sandy, and treeless. These features prompted the Nebraska region to be labeled as the "Great American Desert." As time passed, settlers decided to take on Nebraska's "desert." They began to discover the rich resources the land had to offer.

Nebraska's early pioneers transformed the Great American Desert into farmland. Still, no amount of hard work could turn the exposed rock in the northwest into farmland.

The Pine Ridge area in Nebraska contains 6,600 acres of trees, hills, and rolling plains.

Today, almost the entire state is covered in farms. Thanks to large irrigation systems, land that was once believed too dry for agriculture now yields an abundance of crops. Good soil for farmland has become one of Nebraska's most valuable resources. Also, the state's sand hills and grasslands are now vast grazing ranges that support countless herds of cattle. Nebraska's thriving farmland is not just a source of food, it is also a source of pride for many of the state's residents.

Nebraska is a state of surprising variety. It consists of widespread prairies, hundreds of small lakes, miles of sparkling rivers, dense hand-planted forests, and fascinating rock formations. Nebraskans are closely connected to their environment. The lakes, rivers, sands, prairies, and rolling hills have become part of Nebraska's charming identity and thriving **livelihood**.

QUICK FACTS

Nebraska's state rock is the prairie agate.

Omaha is Nebraska's largest city.

The largest lake in Nebraska is Lake McConaughy at 35,700 surface acres.

Nebraska's state motto is "Equality Before the Law."

There are approximately 56,000 farms in Nebraska.

LAND AND CLIMATE

Nebraska's landscape consists of fertile, rolling plains. These plains are divided into two major land areas. The **Dissected** Till Plains cover the eastern fifth of the state. Several thousand years ago, glaciers blanketed the area. As the glaciers melted, they left behind debris, which served as the basis for extremely fertile soil. Today, the area is made up of lowlands dissected by rivers and streams.

The Great Plains, which is largely grasslands, is another land area in Nebraska. The Sand Hills of the north-central part of the state are an interesting feature of the Great Plains. These vast hills were formed by windblown sand from dried riverbeds. Today, grasses help keep the sand in place.

Nebraska experiences severe seasonal changes. Winters can be bitterly cold, and summers can be uncomfortably hot. The weather can also change quickly. Warm air from the Gulf of Mexico will occasionally collide with cool air from the north, often resulting in wild weather. Tornadoes, blizzards, and violent thunderstorms are all common in the state.

QUICK FACTS

The highest point in Nebraska can be found in Kimball County in the southwest. It is 5,424 feet above sea level.

The lowest recorded temperature in Nebraska was –47°F at Camp Clarke on February 12, 1899. The highest recorded temperature was 118°F at Geneva on July 15, 1934.

There is a region of **badlands** in the state's northwest area. This area consists of deep canyons, sandstone **buttes**, and low, odd-shaped mountains.

Tornadoes in Nebraska often develop from violent thunderstorms.

The Loess Hills in eastern Nebraska
are composed of windblown sand
covering debris from the last Ice Age.

NATURAL RESOURCES

Water is one of Nebraska's greatest natural resources. The state has more than 2,000 small lakes and about 11,000 miles of rivers and streams. It also has one of the largest supplies of underground water in the nation. The Ogallala **aquifer** is an underground reserve of water that stretches as far as Texas. A good portion of this aquifer lies under central Nebraska. Groundwater is pumped to irrigate agricultural land in the region. Water is also stored in the soil. In the Sand Hills, the soil acts like a sponge, absorbing and holding the area's rainfall.

Nebraska has some of the most fertile and productive soil in the world. The land is so ideal for agricultural use that almost 95 percent of it is farmed. Deep deposits of **loess** cover the eastern, central, and south-central parts of the state. Loess forms the basis of some of the best agricultural soils in the country.

Nebraska's farms vary in size. In the Sand Hills and the Panhandle, farms are very large. Farms are much smaller in the eastern part of the state.

The Sand Hills region of Nebraska is about 19,300 square miles in area, and occupies most of north-central Nebraska

PLANTS AND ANIMALS

Because only 2 percent of its land is forested, Nebraska is not well-known for its trees. It is, however, known for its tree-planting. In 1872, Nebraska became the first state to celebrate Arbor Day. A political leader named J. Sterling Morton convinced the state board of agriculture to set aside a day to plant trees on the state's treeless landscape. Morton knew that the roots of the trees would draw much-needed moisture to the soil. In 1885, Arbor Day became a legal holiday in Nebraska, and today it is celebrated in many states throughout the country.

A large portion of Nebraska's hand-planted trees can be found in the Nebraska National Forest. The forest was established in 1902 as an experiment to see if trees could grow in the Sand Hills region. Today, the Bessey Range district of the forest spans 90,000 acres. With about 22,000 acres of the forest planted by hand, it is the largest human-made forest in the western **hemisphere**. There is also a **nursery** in the forest. The Bessey Nursery produces millions of seedlings that are planted in forests across the United States.

Horseback riding is just one of many activities enjoyed in the Nebraska National Forest.

QUICK FACTS

Before it was nicknamed "The Cornhusker State," Nebraska was known as "The Tree Planter State."

Among Nebraska's few trees are pines and cedars, which are commonly found in the western regions. Ashes, cottonwoods, box elders, elms, oaks, walnuts, and willows can all be found in the central and eastern regions of the state.

What Nebraska lacks in trees, it surely makes up for in grasses. It has more varieties of grass than any other state—about 200 species thrive there.

During the spring, evening primroses and violets decorate Nebraska's eastern regions. In the summer, poppies, blue flags, larkspurs, and wild roses blossom in the state.

QUICK FACTS

Cultivation and overgrazing are a constant threat to Nebraska's grasslands. In some parts of the Sand Hills, overgrazing has affected the ability of grasses to grow.

Many fossils can be found at the Agate Fossil Beds National Monument and Toadstool Park.

After Nebraska was opened for settlement, the bison population was almost destroyed. In 1912, J. W. Gilbert offered six bison and seventeen elk to the federal government if land could be found for them. Nebraska's Fort Niobrara National Wildlife Refuge was created, and today the bison, along with many other animals, roam free in the area.

Every spring, the world's largest concentration of sandhill cranes meet in the Platte River Valley.

Millions of years ago, prehistoric animals roamed the Nebraska area. Scientists have uncovered fossil remains in Sioux County in the northwest corner of the state. Fossils of mammoths and **mastodons** have been found there. Other fossils from Sioux County suggest that Nebraska was once a tropical land. **Paleontologists** have uncovered remains of saber-toothed tigers, crocodiles, and rhinoceroses—all of which thrived in tropical climates.

Most of the elk in Nebraska live in the Pine Ridge area. It is estimated that there are more than 200 elk in the state.

Today, Nebraska's wildlife consists mostly of small animals such as badgers, coyotes, foxes, muskrats, jack rabbits, raccoons, skunks, and squirrels. Mule deer also roam much of the region, and antelope and elk are found in the northwest. Game birds such as pheasants, quail, prairie chickens, and wild turkeys are all plentiful in Nebraska's prairies. The state's waters are full of bass, carp, trout, pike, crappies, and perch.

There are large populations of white-tailed deer in Nebraska.

Tourists can visit Railroad Town at the Stuhr Museum of the Prairie Pioneer.

Omaha has its own version of one of England's most famous landmarks. Carhenge, near Alliance, is a re-creation of Stonehenge—but instead of giant stones, it is made out of old cars!

Fort Robinson State Park and Museum was a military post from 1874 to 1948. Today, visitors can sleep in the original and rebuilt buildings.

Omaha's Henry Doorly Zoo is ranked one of the best zoos in the nation. It has a huge aquarium and the world's largest enclosed rain forest. A unique, four-hoofed mammal, called the tapir, can be seen at this zoo.

TOURISM

Every year, thousands of tourists drive through Nebraska on one of the many highways that cross the state. Upon first glance, visitors might conclude that this flat, quiet state has little to offer in the way of sightseeing. They would be mistaken. Nebraska has many wonderful attractions to share. Even its highways are fascinating. Some of the state's highways follow the historic Oregon and Mormon Trails that once led pioneers to the west. In certain places, visitors can look along the roadsides and see the ruts left by the pioneers' wagons.

Nebraska is a great place for history buffs. Several forts and pioneer museums offer a glimpse of what life was like for Nebraska's early settlers. The Stuhr Museum of the Prairie Pioneer allows visitors to relive Nebraska's past with Old West **memorabilia** and Native-American artifacts. There is also a railroad town in the museum that takes visitors back to a time when western towns had wooden sidewalks and posts for tying horses. This town boasts sixty original buildings from the late 1800s. Nebraska brings its history alive for visitors.

Early settlers traveled to Nebraska in covered wagons. Today, visitors to Scott's Bluff National Park can see the old wagon trails.

INDUSTRY

Agriculture is a vital part of Nebraska's economy. There are about 56,000 farms in the state, and each one contributes to the state's position as a leader in this industry. Nebraska ranks second in the nation for its number of beef cattle. Only Texas has more. Hog production is also important to Nebraska's economy. The Cornhusker State is a leading corn producer. It is the third-ranking producer of the country's corn crops. Other crops include soybeans, hay, sorghum, and wheat.

Nebraska's agricultural goods are central to one of the state's other major industries—food processing. The food manufacturing industry uses the state's agricultural products as its **raw materials**. Nebraska is one of the nation's chief producers of meat and grain products. Large meat-packing plants can be found in Dakota City, Fremont, Grand Island, Lexington, Omaha, and Schuler. Breakfast cereal, livestock feed, and bread are all important grain-based products processed in the state.

Livestock and livestock products account for more than 50 percent of Nebraska's farm income.

QUICK FACTS

The first frozen dinner, now known as the TV dinner, was packaged in Omaha in 1953.

Nebraska is a key manufacturer of farm machinery and irrigation equipment. The state also produces chemicals, medicines, and electrical equipment.

A famous type of canned meat, called Spam, is produced in Fremont.

More than half of the state's manufacturing takes place in Omaha and Lincoln.

Beef sales make up 80 percent of Nebraska's livestock income.

Coal makes up much of the freight transported through Nebraska. The state has the largest freight rail yard in the world.

GOODS AND SERVICES

Nebraska's central location is responsible for its thriving transportation industry. For hundreds of years, people have used the Platte River Valley as a transportation route. In 1865, Omaha became the eastern **terminus** of the first transcontinental railroad in the United States. Railroad companies then began laying track westward, making Omaha an important center for railroad transport. Today, the Union Pacific Railroad has its headquarters in Omaha, and three major rail lines provide freight service to the state.

Omaha is not only one of the nation's chief rail centers, it is also a powerful financial center. Many of the country's largest insurance companies and **telemarketing** companies have their head offices there. Lincoln is also an important insurance center and a leading **wholesale** and retail trade center.

QUICK FACTS

Farm products account for almost 70 percent of Nebraska's outgoing freight.

Although Nebraska has many rivers, only the Missouri River is useful for shipping. Along the Missouri, Omaha is the principal shipping port, but ports in Nebraska City and South Sioux City are also active.

Real estate is a major economic activity in Nebraska. The buying and selling of farms, houses, and other large properties generates large sums of money in the state.

Nebraska has a strong telemarketing industry.

Many Nebraskans have jobs with the government. Government services in the state include the operation of electrical utilities, public hospitals, and military bases. The headquarters of the United States Strategic Command (USSTRATCOM) are on the Offutt Air Force Base near Omaha. The Command Center controls the country's bombers and long-range missiles.

With a large number of teachers working at the state's schools, the public school system is a major employer in Nebraska. Students are given many opportunities for higher learning in the state. The University of Nebraska, which opened in 1871, has campuses in three different locations. Students can choose from campuses in Omaha, Lincoln, and Kearney. Other major universities and colleges throughout the state offer programs of study in a variety of fields. Among these schools are Peru State College, Nebraska Wesleyan University, Bellevue University, and Creighton University.

There are more than 20,000 students enrolled at the Lincoln campus of the University of Nebraska.

The Omaha lived in earth lodges during spring and summer. Earth lodges had a dome-shaped roof and were about 8 feet high.

QUICK FACTS

The discovery of fragments of ancient stone tools and weapons suggests that people were living in the Nebraska area at least 10,000 years ago. Very little is known about these first peoples.

In the mid-1600s, horses were introduced to the Native Peoples of Nebraska. Horses changed their lives. They were able to hunt game with better speed and efficiency.

Some Native Peoples moved to Nebraska because settlers drove them from their homes in the east. The Winnebago, who originally lived in Wisconsin, moved to Nebraska in the early 1860s.

FIRST NATIONS

In the 1700s, European explorers made their way to Nebraska and found several groups of Native Peoples. Many groups who lived along the rivers farmed and hunted. Among these peaceful peoples were the Mission, Omaha, Oto, and Ponca. The Pawnee were the largest group to settle along Nebraska's Platte, Republican, and Loup rivers. They hunted and farmed, but unlike their neighbors, they were not peaceful. The Pawnee fought with the Sioux and the Comanche, who both lived in the west of the state.

The groups in western Nebraska relied mostly on hunting for their livelihood. The Sioux, Comanche, Cheyenne, and Arapaho were all **nomadic** peoples. They lived in temporary villages, following and hunting buffalo and other game. Because their livelihood depended on hunting, these groups worked together to defend their hunting grounds against the Pawnee and early settlers.

The Lakota had seven different bands, and each was headed by a chief.

Father Flanagan's Home for Boys offered new, positive approaches for dealing with troubled youth.

QUICK FACTS

Nebraska's most well known missionary was Father Edward Joseph Flanagan. In 1917, he founded Father Flanagan's Home for Boys in Omaha. This was a home and school for neglected or troubled boys. The home was moved west of Omaha in 1918, and quickly became incorporated as Boys Town.

Spanish explorer Francisco Vasquez de Coronado ventured as far as Kansas, just south of Nebraska. When he claimed the territory, which included present-day Nebraska, he had never even seen the area.

Spain objected to France's exploration of the Nebraska region. The Spanish felt they controlled the area. In 1720, a Spanish expedition tried to stop the French, but was defeated by a group of Pawnees.

EXPLORERS AND MISSIONARIES

In 1541, a Spanish explorer named Francisco Vasquez de Coronado led an expedition across southwestern United States. Coronado claimed a large area for Spain, which included present-day Nebraska. Over one hundred years later, René-Robert Cavelier, known as Sieur de La Salle, traveled down the Mississippi River. He claimed all the land drained by the Mississippi River for France. Cavelier named this vast area Louisiana after his king, Louis XIV. By the end of the seventeenth century, both Spain and France had claimed the Nebraska region without ever having set foot in the area.

The first recorded European to enter Nebraska was a French explorer named Etienne Veniard de Bourgmont. In 1714, he traveled up the Missouri River to the mouth of the Platte and built a trading post. Other French pioneers followed, but more local exploration was to come. In 1803, the United States bought France's lands in North America in the Louisiana Purchase. Soon after, President Thomas Jefferson sent Meriwether Lewis and William Clark to explore the territory.

Many early trading posts developed into Nebraska's first towns.

EARLY SETTLERS

United States explorers and fur traders soon followed Lewis and Clark to the Nebraska wilderness. In the early 1800s, several trading posts were built along the Missouri River. Native Peoples in the area felt that their land was being threatened. The United States government built Fort Atkinson to prevent potential clashes. Construction of the fort began in 1819, bringing hundreds of United States soldiers to the region. Fort Atkinson became the site of Nebraska's first school, library, sawmill, and **gristmill**.

By the 1840s, pioneers were traveling through Nebraska on their way to the fertile farmlands of Oregon. Even though thousands of people trudged through Nebraska at this time, no one settled in the area. Even if pioneers had wanted to settle there, they would not have been allowed. The United States government had declared the region Native-American land, and only Native Peoples, missionaries, and licensed traders were allowed to live in the area.

The Bordeaux Trading Post was in use from 1837 to 1876. Today, it is a museum that preserves the history of the fur trade.

QUICK FACTS

The American Fur Trading Company built many trading posts during the 1820s. Bellevue, where one of these posts was established, became Nebraska's first permanent settlement.

Fort Atkinson was abandoned eight years after it was built when the government was sure that peace had been established between settlers and Native Peoples.

Fort Atkinson was the first fort that was built west of the Missouri River. At the time, it was the largest military post in the United States. It is now a historical park.

Plattsmouth was so named because the city was situated at the mouth of the Platte River.

One of the first farms to be claimed under the Homestead Act was near Beatrice. Daniel Freeman claimed it in 1863.

Since Nebraska was first settled, agriculture has been the driving force behind the state's economy.

The Union Pacific Railway began laying track westward from Omaha in 1865. The Union Pacific and the Burlington Railways campaigned to bring more settlers to Nebraska. The companies sent pamphlets describing the Nebraska farmland to people living in the eastern states and in Europe. This offer brought many people to the Nebraska area.

In 1854, the United States government passed the Kansas-Nebraska Act. This act created the Kansas and Nebraska territories and opened the region for settlement. Settlers from the eastern states began to arrive. Nebraska's first towns sprang up along or near the Missouri River. By 1860, there were more than 28,000 people living in the region.

The Homestead Act of 1862 brought a rush of eager pioneers to the Nebraska territory. The act granted 160 free acres of western **frontier** to any settler who wished to farm it. Settlers would own the land after they had farmed it for five years. This offer encouraged thousands of homesteaders to make their way to Nebraska. During the late 1800s, the new farmers had plenty of bad luck. They suffered through some very cold winters and long periods of drought. There was also a brief period when swarms of grasshoppers plagued the area, ruining crops. Discouraged, many farmers left the plains. Still, others remained, and before long, improved farming techniques brought more settlers to Nebraska.

With few trees in the Nebraska region, early settlers had to build their homes with sod. These settlers were nicknamed "Sodbusters."

POPULATION

Historic Haymarket in downtown Lincoln is known for its many restaurants and retail stores.

Nebraska has about 1.7 million people. In the early 1900s, almost 70 percent of Nebraskans lived in rural areas. As time passed, this number shifted dramatically. Many people left the rural areas because of the growing employment opportunities in the state's towns and cities. Today, most Nebraskans live in urban areas. The population is especially dense around the state's two largest cities, Omaha and Lincoln. More than half of all Nebraskans live in these two **metropolitan** areas.

Nebraska's urban areas are almost all located in the eastern part of the state, although a few densely populated areas can be found along the Platte and North Platte Rivers. Some north and central areas of the state are sparsely populated. In fact, some counties have an average of less than five residents per square mile.

QUICK FACTS

Omaha and Lincoln are less than 60 miles apart.

The largest county in the United States is Nebraska's Cherry County. The largest community in Cherry County has just under 3,000 people.

Omaha has about 370,000 people within the city limits, but the whole metropolitan area of Omaha has about 687,000. Lincoln has 213,000 people.

After Omaha and Lincoln, Nebraska's largest cities are Grand Island, Bellevue, Kearney, Fremont, North Platte, and Hastings.

Omaha is the commercial, manufacturing, and telecommunications center of Nebraska.

Nebraska's Capitol began construction in 1922. It took ten years to complete and cost about $10 million.

POLITICS AND GOVERNMENT

Nebraska's government is unique among all the states in the nation. Like most other states, Nebraska has an executive branch of government that is headed by a governor. It also has a lieutenant governor, secretary of state, attorney general, and treasurer. All are elected to four-year terms. Also like the other states, Nebraska has a judicial system that is headed by a Supreme Court. But Nebraska is the only state in the Union to have a **unicameral** legislature.

Nebraska's legislature was not always unicameral. The state had a bicameral legislature, with both a Senate and a House of Representatives, for sixty-eight years. Then, in 1934, Nebraskans voted to rid themselves of half their state legislature. People felt that a unicameral formation would be more democratic and more open to the public than a bicameral system. In 1937, Nebraska's first session of unicameral legislature was held. Today, there are forty-nine members in the legislature. These members are referred to as senators, and each of them serves a term of four years.

QUICK FACTS

Nebraska has ninety-three counties, each with a clerk, sheriff, and a treasurer.

Gerald Ford, born in Omaha, became vice president of the United States under President Nixon. In 1974, Ford became the thirty-eighth president of the United States when Nixon resigned from office.

Gerald Ford

Nebraska is the only state in the nation to have a nonpartisan legislature. This means that the state's legislative leadership has no connection to political parties.

The Saunders Courthouse in Wahoo is about 100 years old.

Wausa honors its Swedish heritage with the Wausa Community Swedish Smorgasbord.

CULTURAL GROUPS

During the nineteenth century, thousands of Europeans came to Nebraska in search of free or inexpensive land to farm. German, Swedish, Czech, Irish, and Italian **immigrants** flocked to the region. Today, a large portion of Nebraska's population are their descendants. Many of them work hard to preserve the special cultural traditions of their ancestors.

A large number of the state's ethnic communities are concentrated in specific villages or towns. The village of Wausa, for example, has many people of Swedish descent. The Wausa Community Swedish Smorgasbord is held every October. For more than fifty years, the event has celebrated Swedish traditions with colorful costumes, food, and music. In Wilbur, the annual National Czech Festival showcases Czech culture with arts, crafts, and food. Czech dancers and musicians are featured in daily parades.

The Wilber Czech Museum displays Czech history and culture. It has an outstanding collection of dolls, costumes, laces, and replicas of early immigrant homes.

CZECH CAPITAL OF THE

Nebraska's Native Americans actively preserve and share their cultural traditions through colorful and lively **powwow** celebrations. Powwows feature traditional dancing, foods, and beadwork. During the first full moon in August, the Omaha Tribe of Nebraska hosts a powwow to celebrate the harvest. This powwow is the oldest harvest celebration in the state. Also, the Winnebago in Nebraska hold their annual powwow in July.

There are many events and sites throughout Nebraska that pay tribute to the state's heritage. Cowboy museums in Gordon and Ogallala recognize the ranching traditions and activities that continue to be a large part of Nebraska life. Pioneer museums, festivals, and landmarks showcase Nebraska's important historic figures and events. Many people honor their state with special events. Every year in Lincoln, Nebraskans celebrate their state during the Nebraska State Fair, which features Nebraskan talent, including local arts and crafts.

Many Sioux attend powwows in Nebraska during the summer.

QUICK FACTS

Native Americans make up about 1 percent of Nebraska's population.

The Dancing Leaf Earth Lodge Cultural Center is located south of Wellfleet. At this lodge, visitors can learn about the lives of early Native Peoples.

Dannebrog is the Danish capital of Nebraska. Danish heritage is celebrated in June with Danish Day, or Grundlovs Fest.

Susette La Flesche was the daughter of an Omaha chief. She fought for the rights of Native Peoples and wrote many stories about their lives.

Septemberfest is a popular annual attraction in Omaha.

More than 200,000 people see the Omaha Symphony perform each year.

ARTS AND ENTERTAINMENT

Many popular entertainers are from the state of Nebraska. Famous actors such as Marlon Brando, Nick Nolte, and the late Henry Fonda all hail from the Cornhusker State. Other famous Cornhuskers include comedian Johnny Carson and the late Fred Astaire, an actor and dancer during the 1930s and 1940s.

Nebraska's entertainment scene is not limited to the Cornhuskers who left for Hollywood and Broadway. The state supports many impressive theatrical troupes and programs for theater, music, and dance lovers. Omaha is a major center for the arts in Nebraska. Among this city's theaters are the Omaha Theater Company for Young People and the Omaha Magic Theater. The Omaha Community Playhouse is the largest community theater in the United States, and boasts a professional touring company called the Nebraska Theater Caravan. The Orpheum Theater is home to the Omaha Symphony and the Ballet Omaha. The Orpheum also houses Opera Omaha, one of the nation's most progressive opera companies.

QUICK FACTS

The Omaha Theater Company for Young People is the third-largest professional theater for children in the country.

Harold Lloyd, born in Buchard, was a comedian during the silent movie era. He did his own stunts. In his movie *Safety Last* he dangled from a clock on a skyscraper!

In 1938, a movie was made about Nebraska's Home for Boys, called *Boys Town.* Actor Spencer Tracy won an Academy Award for his performance as Father Flanagan.

Marlon Brando, an actor from Omaha, won Academy Awards for his roles in *The Godfather* and *On the Waterfront*.

The Lied Center for Performing Arts brings some of the world's best arts and entertainment to the people of Lincoln.

The Nebraska Jazz Orchestra presents many concerts in Lincoln and Omaha.

Nebraska's most famous author is Willa Cather, who moved to Nebraska at the age of nine. She wrote novels about pioneer life on Nebraska's prairies. Willa Cather died in 1947.

The performing arts thrive in other parts of the state, too. The Lincoln Community Playhouse puts on engaging performances, and the Lincoln Civic Orchestra entertains listeners with musical works. The Lied Center for Performing Arts at the University of Nebraska in Lincoln presents nationally and internationally recognized performers. Many of Nebraska's smaller cities and towns have strong music and theater programs at their universities and colleges.

Nebraska is as rich in visual arts as it is in performing arts. Omaha's Joslyn Art Museum has one of the finest Western art collections in the country. It also has exhibits of classic and modern works, all of which are housed in a beautiful marble building. The Sheldon Memorial Art Gallery and Sculpture Garden is on the grounds of Lincoln's University of Nebraska. It has fascinating displays of twentieth-century North American paintings and beautiful displays of sculpture. The Museum of Nebraska Art in Kearney has twelve galleries, some of which showcase works of art by talented Nebraskans.

Nebraska's Joslyn Art Museum is a center for cultural activities. It is the site of music concerts, dance recitals, lectures, and workshops.

The Buffalo Bill Wild West Show was one of the most successful and entertaining rodeo shows in the 1800s.

SPORTS

Nebraska is known for its rodeos. The state's first rodeo was put on in the 1880s by William "Buffalo Bill" Cody. Buffalo Bill was one of the most well-known cowboys from the Old West. He was a famous **Pony Express** rider, army scout, and buffalo hunter. In 1882, the town officials of North Platte asked Buffalo Bill to put together a special celebration for the Fourth of July. What he organized is thought to be the first official rodeo in the nation. Today, the Buffalo Bill Rodeo is held every June near the town of North Platte. It features local cowboy talent.

There are many other rodeos throughout the state. Nebraska's Biggest Rodeo is held each July in Burwell. In fact, Burwell's rodeo grounds are active all summer long with ranch rodeos and professional rodeos. There are several other county and community rodeos held throughout the state.

QUICK FACTS

Lincoln is home to the National Museum of Roller Skating. The museum has the world's largest collection of roller skates and roller-skating memorabilia. It also has displays on roller disco, trick skaters, and skating animals.

The forests and rugged rock formations in Nebraska's Pine Ridge area are popular destinations for hikers, cyclists, and campers.

The Burwell Rodeo draws about 15,000 visitors through its gates each year.

Women athletes at Nebraska State University have been thrilling fans for more than twenty-five years.

Nebraskans have no major league sports teams to cheer on, but their commitment to college athletics is outstanding. The University of Nebraska recruits and trains some of the finest young athletes in the country. A number of Cornhuskers teams compete against other college teams in volleyball, basketball, baseball, and other team sports.

The college football season draws the most lively and enthusiastic Nebraskan fans. The Cornhuskers are a strong football team and have finished many seasons as one of the top ten teams in the country. They have also won numerous Big Ten championships. When at home, the team plays at the University of Nebraska's Memorial Stadium in Lincoln, where loyal fans pack the stadium. Season tickets to Cornhuskers games are as valued in Nebraska as season tickets to major league football games are in other states.

The Nebraska Cornhuskers football team holds the record for most points scored in a Bowl game.

Brain Teasers

1

TRUE OR FALSE?

The world's largest mammoth fossil was found in Nebraska.

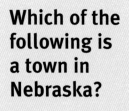

Answer: True. The mammoth stood almost 135 feet tall.

2

TRUE OR FALSE?

Nebraska's Cherry County is larger than the state of Connecticut.

Answer: True

3

Which of the following is a town in Nebraska?

a) Friend

b) Beaver City

c) Wahoo

d) All of the above

Answer: d

4

One of Nebraska's biggest festivals and rodeos is the Ak-Sar-Ben. What is special about that name?

Answer: Ak-Sar-Ben is "Nebraska" spelled backwards.

5

What tasty beverage was invented in Nebraska?

a) Orange Crush

b) Root Beer

c) Kool-Aid

d) Chocolate Milk

Answer: c. Edward E. Perkins of Hastings invented Kool-Aid in 1927.

6

TAKE A GUESS!

What famous system of emergency communication was first developed and used in Nebraska?

Answer: The 911 emergency telephone number.

7

TRUE OR FALSE?

The building that houses the Mutual of Omaha's headquarters in Nebraska has no basement.

Answer: False. The public building was actually built with seven of its floors underground.

8

Where were the world's first test-tube tigers raised?

Answer: The Henry Doorly Zoo in Omaha.

FOR MORE INFORMATION

Books

Fradin, Dennis Brindell. *Nebraska.* From the Sea to Shining Sea series. Chicago: Children's Press, 1995.

Hargrove, Jim. *Nebraska.* From the America the Beautiful series. Chicago: Children's Press, 1989.

Porter, A.P. *Hello USA: Nebraska.* Minneapolis: Lerner Group, 1991.

Web sites

You can also go online and have a look at the following Web sites:

Official site of the State of Nebraska
http://www.state.ne.us

Nebraska Tourism
http://www.visitnebraska.org

Nebraska Unicameral
http://www.unicam.state.ne.us

Henry Doorly Zoo
http://www.omahazoo.com

Some Web sites stay current longer than others. To find other Nebraska Web sites, enter search terms such as "Nebraska," "Omaha," "Cornhusker State," or any other topic you want to research.

GLOSSARY

aquifer: a formation of rock that soaks up moisture to form large reserves of groundwater

badlands: a barren area with interesting rock formations

buttes: isolated hills or mountains rising above the surrounding land

corridor: land that links two areas or that follows a road or river

dissected: divided by river valleys

frontier: land that forms the furthest boundary of inhabited regions

gristmill: a mill that grinds grain

hemisphere: half of the globe

hydroelectric: water-generated electricity

immigrants: people who move to a new country

irrigation: to supply dry land with water through human-made processes, such as by channeling streams

livelihood: means of financial support

loess: a yellowish sandy deposit that is carried by wind

mastodons: large, extinct, elephant-like mammals

memorabilia: souvenirs

metropolitan: large or busy urban areas

nomadic: having no permanent home; moving from place to place in search of food

nursery: a place where young plants and trees are grown for planting elsewhere

paleontologists: scientists who study prehistoric remains, such as fossils

Pony Express: a system of mail delivery that was popular in the mid-1800s. Mail carriers would ride ponies between Missouri and California, delivering messages

powwow: a Native-American ceremony

raw materials: materials, taken from the land, that have not been processed

sod: a piece of earth, usually covered in grass or roots

telemarketing: selling or marketing things over the telephone

terminus: the end of a railroad route

unicameral: a legislature that consists of only one house

wholesale: the selling of goods in large quantities

INDEX